Ta

1. Genesis

2. My first successful deer hunt

3. Fulfilling the dream of a buffalo hunt

4. An Oklahoma Deer Hunt

5. Kansas Duck Hunt with a 5-month-old Chesapeake Bay Retriever

6. First Oklahoma muzzleloader deer hunt

7. Remembering a Ft. Benning hog and deer drive

8. Hunting the Kansas Rut-What a surprise!!

Genesis

This first story is called *"Genesis"* as it explains my simple beginnings as a hunter. A lot of experiences come to mind when I think back over the 30 plus years that I've been hunting. Unlike most hunters, and perhaps just like you, I did not come from a hunting family. Daddy didn't hunt and it was just recently that my parents finally stopped wondering where in the world I came from. The running joke in the family is that they must have gone waaaay back in the family tree to get me. After all, I was indeed different. Unlike most Black kids, I didn't care too much about sports. Sure, I played basketball in the backyard with cousins and friends, and pretended that I was Larry Bird or Magic Johnson, but my love was for fishing, hunting, guns, and everything outdoors.

It seems like it was yesterday when I, at the age of 4 or 5, was on the back porch of my grandparents' house in the country, watching a rabbit eating at the edge of the yard. This was the same little white house where Daddy and his 11 siblings were raised. One of Daddy's older brothers, Uncle John L, was there with my grandparents. I said "Look, a rabbit!" Uncle John L asked me if I wanted him to shoot it for me and of course I said "Yes". Uncle John L reached inside the screen door, pulled out a single shot, or single barrel shotgun as most people called them then, took aim, and shot the rabbit. That was my first time seeing an animal killed. It didn't bother me one bit, because I didn't care about the rabbit, I wanted the shotgun shell and snatched it up as soon as it landed on the porch. "Go get that rabbit boy" Uncle John L told me, but that wasn't happening. At 4 or 5 years old I wanted no part of touching a dead rabbit, or a live one either for that matter. I can remember Uncle John L going out and picking up the rabbit, me watching him clean it, and all of us eating the rabbit after my grandmother fried it for us. I guess that this could technically be considered my first hunt, but it would be decades before I would actually shoot an animal on my own.

My earliest memories of the hunt take me back to 1982 when I was 11 or 12 years old. Not allowed to own a real gun, I terrorized the squirrels and birds in my neighborhood with my Crossman 760 Pumpmaster, the pellet gun that Daddy taught me to shoot with. After a lot of pestering and getting on my Daddy's nerves to take me hunting, he finally gave in and bought a Marlin bolt-action .22 caliber rifle with a 7 shot detachable magazine, a gun that he still has to this day. I vividly remember my first "real" hunt which took place on another one of his brother's land, Uncle Robert. Uncle Robert's son, Quienten was about 9 or 10 and had also come along with us. He had a full-sized pump action 12 gauge that was nearly as tall as he was. I remember how terribly nervous Daddy was with my cousin toting that shotgun around, and now that I'm 45 years old, I can understand why. That day we ended up with one squirrel that Daddy shot in the hip.

Using my neighborhood as my primary hunting grounds, it didn't take long to figure out that squirrels are tough little critters, but I learned that head shots and behind the shoulder shots with a .177 caliber pellet would dispatch a squirrel quite nicely at close range. One Christmas when I was about 13 or 14, Daddy gave me a $50 bill as a Christmas present. I thought I was rich! That money was burning a hole in my pocket, and I could not wait for Daddy to carry me up the street to K-Mart to look at their selection of pellet guns. Sure, I wanted a .22 rifle or a .410 shotgun, but my parents were not having it. They told me that I would just get into trouble if I had a real gun, and flat out refused to buy me one. So I had to resort to the next best thing.

In the sporting goods department of Kmart, I found a Crossman 2100 Classic. To me, this was like the Holy Grail of pellet guns and a huge upgrade from the 760. While the 760 Pumpmaster fired BBs at 625 feet per second and .177 pellets at 600 feet per second, the 2100 Classic could fire BBs at 755 feet per second and .177 pellets at 725 feet per second. I thought that this was serious squirrel and bird medicine. Yes, I hunted songbirds like most kids did in those days although I now realize how wrong it was. Back then, I had to satisfy my urge to hunt something, and I knew every bird in our part of the State just by the sounds they made.

I knew a Blue Jay from a Thrash, a Thrash from a Boston Oriole, a Boston Oriole from a Robin, and so on. I considered buying a .22 caliber pellet gun but the higher velocities of the .177 caliber pellet always seemed more impressive to me. Plus the .22 caliber pellets and air guns were not as popular as the .177 caliber guns. At the time, I knew nothing about kinetic energy and the facts surrounding the physics of a heavier grained pellet moving at slower speeds, but delivering superior penetration and knockdown power. For me it was always about the speed. I had seen Benjamin and Sherman air rifles in the Sears & Roebuck catalog, and knew that they were serious air rifles, but considering that they cost well over $100, even back in the 80's, they were out of my price range.

As mentioned before, I did not come from a hunting family but there were two hunters in my family that stand out in my mind- Uncle John L and James Williams. James Williams was an older cousin that was the same age as my parents. Uncle John L had slowed down with his hunting by the time that I was of hunting age, and had settled into small scale farming and raising rabbits. He had hunted deer in his younger years and his rifle of choice was a Winchester model 1894 chambered in .44 Magnum. I remember that before he moved inside the city limits he had a small shack out in the country, down near Childersburg, AL where he raised a hog or two for slaughtering. One day Uncle John L was preparing to kill a hog for winter and Daddy carried me down to see the action. I guess to show me what it was like when he was growing up as a child. Another guy was there and he was the one that was going to do the shooting. I can remember it like yesterday, I must have been about 12 or 13 and I asked Uncle John L how was he going to kill it. He said that he was going to put a little corn on the ground and the other guy would shoot it between the eyes. That hog looked huge to me, at least 300lbs. It was common for folks to fatten up hogs before killing them and I knew more than a few people who kept slop buckets at their house for their hogs. Forever intrigued by guns, I asked what kind of gun was the guy going to use and was shocked to hear that he was using a .22. I thought that he would say a .30-30 or shotgun but nope; he said a ".22". I also remember the guy taking out a handful of .22 cartridges out of his pocket and showing them to me. He said that the week prior he had to shoot a hog several times in order to kill it, so this time he came prepared. With the corn on the ground, the hog walked up to the edge of the pen, started feeding, then "Pirrr!!" the guy put a bullet right between the hogs' eyes causing it to drop in its tracks. That was the first time I saw a big game animal killed and the first time I saw how quickly somebody could move in to cut off a set of hog testicles. Where I grew up, they called hog testicles "mountain oysters" and they were said to be used as an aphrodisiac by the men folk. I also remember Uncle John L doing a little target practicing with his .38 snub nose that day. He was shooting at an oil can, yes, oil came in cans back then. He asked if I wanted to shoot the .38. I told him yes, but Daddy said no. He said that I was too young and maybe when I'm older. You see, us kids, all of us cousins, boys and girls, loved Uncle John L because you had fun when you were around Uncle John L. He would let you shoot guns, touch guns, tell you stories about hunting, stories of his hunting dogs, tell you fishing stories and would even give you a sip of whiskey or a pinch of chewing tobacco if you wanted it. His actions would definitely land him in jail in today's time. He would likely be charged with contributing to the delinquency of a minor, but a little sip of whiskey or a pinch of Redman chewing tobacco ain't never hurt nobody. It didn't matter if you were a boy or a girl, Uncle John L would offer you a pinch of tobacco in a minute, and all of us kids turned out to be just fine in life. I'm sure that some of y'all had a relative like Uncle John L.

My cousin James Williams was also a die-hard hunter and remained a die- hard hunter well into his 70's. Growing up, James Williams, we never seemed to call him by just his first name, spent a lot of time hunting with groups of other hunters. In fact, he was hunting with a diverse group of hunters, yes Blacks and Whites, in the 1970's- in Alabama. James Williams was an avid deer and rabbit hunter who loved the .270 Winchester as a deer caliber. After realizing that my love and interest in guns and hunting was a permanent part of my identity, my parents suggested that I go hunting with James Williams.

"Eric, why don't you go hunting with James Williams?" they'd ask. I declined. At the time I viewed hunting as a solitary activity, or one that was best done with father and son. It would be years before I realized the fun and benefits of hunting as part of a group or party. But it would not be until 2011 that I would finally go deer hunting with James Williams. I think at this time he was 74 years old, still climbing 15-20 feet up a tree in a climbing tree stand.

This is just the beginning of how I got started hunting, and I will admit that while it was not the traditional way when compared to other hunters, it made me the hunter that I am today. To date I've hunted multiple species of game and have hunted 22 of the 50 states. I have also hunted South Africa. In future memories of the hunt, I will share my pursuit of deer, turkey, buffalo, snow geese, hogs, duck, African plains game, upland bird, caribou on the Alaskan tundra, and more! Some hunts were successful, some were not, but you will hear them all. Each story will include three lessons learned from the hunt. This first story is called *Genesis* as it explains my simple beginnings as a hunter. The final chapter, "*Omega*", will hopefully be published several decades from now when I'm old and grey, have taught others everything that I know about hunting, and am at the end of my life as a hunter. Until that day comes, enjoy the memories from my hunts and let them serve as entertainment as well as inspiration. Thanks for purchasing this book and enjoy the dozens of stories to come! Eric.

The author at the age of 5 with his first fish.

My first successful deer hunt!

Deer hunting is the most popular type of big game hunting in America. It is definitely the most advertised. With millions of deer roaming the U.S, and with almost every hunting magazine showcasing big trophy bucks, it's no wonder that many aspiring hunters dream of hunting deer.

Unlike many hunters, I did not come from a hunting family. Daddy wasn't a hunter. So, getting my first deer took about 12 years of trial, error, disappointment, frustration, and bumping a lot of deer as I tromped through the woods. As a child, I honed my shooting skills on songbirds and squirrels that lived around my neighborhood, in those days it was nothing to see kids roaming the neighborhood woods with air rifles in search of squirrels. I started chasing deer at the age of 18, but unfortunately was hunting them as if I was looking for squirrels, meaning that I would tromp through the woods having zero clue about stealth, wind direction, movement, or anything that I should be paying attention to,in order to be successful. Needless to say, I rarely saw a deer while in the woods. If I did, it was the back end of one with the white tail raised high, bounding off through the woods. I had no clue what I was doing.

Fast forward to 2001, shortly after my parents built a new home in the country which was surrounded by hundreds of acres of land. Deer, turkey, squirrels, quail, and other game were everywhere. I knew that it was just a matter of time before I had a successful hunt. Each time I would come home to visit, I would hit the woods in search of deer, only to repeat the failures of past years. I would see deer but only after I had already been smelled or spotted. There were tracks and deer sign everywhere. I just had to find a way to get a shot at one.

One cool morning during the '98 or '99 Alabama deer season, I was in the woods again armed with the only centerfire rifle that I owned, a surplus SKS Chinese rifle chambered in 7.62x39. I had two types of ammunition for that rifle, full metal jacket (FMJ) and hollow points (HP). Since it was illegal to hunt with full metal jacketed ammunition, I had the gun loaded with 123 grain hollow points. It was Russian surplus ammo that I had gotten at Mike's Army surplus store there in Talladega. The price was about $2.00 for a box of 20 rounds. On previous hunting trips, I had notice an area along a gas pipeline where the deer had a well-worn trail leading from the woods, onto the edge of the pipeline. This pipeline was a mowed path about three car lanes wide, that went on for miles. I had made a simple blind out of burlap and boards, with a chair to sit in. On the morning of the hunt I got up early, before the crack of dawn, and walked across the yard to the pipeline, then down about 100 yards. I surely hoped that I would see a deer. Settling into my blind, I got to see another beautiful sunrise and heard the woods come alive. It seems as if birds start stirring at the first hint of sunrise. After sitting for an hour or so, I caught movement to my right, forty yards away, at about a 45-degree angle. It was a deer, a doe! Like most new deer hunters who have never shot a deer, my heart started beating 100 beats a minute, excitement shot through my body as I shuffled to get into a shooting position. The distance was only about 40 yards and the deer was coming my way. It seemed like there were other deer behind it, but it didn't matter. I had my eyes, and now rifle sights, on this one, and it looked like I was finally, finally, going to get myself a deer after all these years! The doe wasn't a big one, but that was okay, because a small deer was better than no deer. As the deer closed the distance to about 25 yards, it turned broadside giving me a perfect shot at its shoulder. I took careful aim with my SKS and fired. "Boom!" The shot echoed out across the pipeline. The bullet found its mark and the doe jumped straight into the air upon feeling the impact of the bullet. She ran about 20 yards down the pipeline in a full sprint, then turned into the woods. "Yes!! I got it! Whoo hoo!!! I'm the man, I'm the man!" Yes, I got it!" I was so excited.

Finally, after 14 years of trial and error, I had finally gotten a deer! I jumped up and ran over to where the deer was standing when I shot it. I saw blood, a decent blood trail. I tracked it down the pipeline and into the woods, I was moving as fast as I could go. Once I got about 10 yards inside the woods, the blood trail led me to a tree with a plate sized pool of matted bloody pine straw. It looked as if the deer had laid down. But the blood trail continued, and I was hot on the trail determined to find that deer. As I tracked on for another 15 minutes or so, I was wondering why I had not come upon the deer. The blood trail was good, and I could not understand why I had not found it yet. It seemed as if the trail was going on forever, deeper into the woods, places I had never been. Places I didn't know existed. At one point I lost the trail and had no idea where the deer went. I clapped my hands loudly and hollered hoping that I would force the deer to move if it was somewhere close and still alive. Sure enough, it was still alive as I saw a white tail, also known as the white flag, bounding ahead of me.

"Man, why isn't this deer dead?" I thought as I walked over to where I saw the deer running.

Yep, it was the same deer, as was evident by a now faint but visible blood trail. Instead of solid drips and puddles of blood, I was now seeing small drops and specks here and there. Then I didn't see anything. As I wandered through the woods, I came across a clearing with grass and shrubs about knee high. It was a nice-looking area as if it had been clear cut a few years earlier. Could the deer be in here? I clapped my hands and hollered again, hoping to make the deer show itself. Scanning the clearing, I didn't see anything. Suddenly I caught a glimpse of something that moved. It was an ear. As I forced my eyes to focus, and make sense of what I was seeing, it was the deer! It was bedded down about 25 yards from me, looking directly at me. It was blended in so well that I had looked right past it.

Taking careful aim, I fired a shot into the deer's neck, which ended my chase.

As I walked over to the deer, I was shocked to find out that it was not a "she", it was a "he". It was not a doe, instead, it was a "button buck". For those that don't know, a "button buck" is a young male deer that is just starting to grow its antlers, but the antlers have not grown through the skin. They look like two buttons on top of his head. In some parts of the country, they call them "nubbin bucks". Welp, I still had a deer, a yearling, but I was proud of it and could not wait to get it back to my parent's house for them to see. At this point I was clearly lost, but I grabbed the deer by the back leg and started dragging it towards the pipeline, which I thought was in front of me a few hundred yards. Coming out to the pipeline, I saw a paved road that I never knew existed. The only paved road I knew around here was the one that my parents lived off of, but this road was to my right instead of being to my left, I realized that I had to go left towards the house so off I went, dragging the deer and toting the SKS. At this time I was a younger man and in good physical condition, but I had to take several breaks along the way. After 30 minutes or so of dragging the deer, I saw the familiar paved road ahead, and my daddy standing out in the middle of the pipeline.

"Hey I heard you shoot earlier. Did you get something?" he asked.

"Yes sir, I got a deer!" I told him as I drug the deer to him, proud as I could be.

"A deer?" he asked in amazement.

"Yep, a deer." I told him.

    You see, for years I had been going hunting and coming home empty-handed. I'd come home and my parents would ask me the same question.

"Get anything?" And the answer would always be, "Nope", I saw one, or "Well I got a squirrel".

But this time, I was able to say "Yes I got a deer!".

"I hollered for you, but I guess that you couldn't hear me". Daddy told me.

"Yeah, I was waaay down the pipeline. I was almost to the next road which is almost a mile down the pipeline." I told him.

    Daddy helped me get the deer to the house where we took pictures and hung him up on a tree so that we could skin it. I had helped several guys skin a deer before, their deer, after their successful hunt, but I had never done one by myself. Daddy, not being a hunter, but having been raised in the country where they raised hogs, knew how to skin and clean a hog.

"Well Son, I guess that you would clean this deer the same as you would a hog." he told me as we started cutting on it. So between the both of us, we managed to get the deer skinned, gutted, and quartered; which is a fancy way of saying that we cut it up and put it into the cooler. Daddy wanted to cut the throat like they did on the hogs back in the day, but I told him that it was no need to do that. There wasn't much blood left in him, based on how much the deer had bled out.

The whole neighborhood knew that I had gotten a deer. Family members, cousins, friends of the family, the birds, the mailman, everybody! Why? Because my parents and I told them. That afternoon as I sat around reliving the hunt, and telling my parents step by step what happened, again and again, I was relieved to have finally, finally, gotten my first deer - at the ripe old age of 30!

The three lessons learned from this hunt were:

1. **Do not use hollow points or fast expanding bullets on deer-** Hollow points are not the best deer hunting bullet. Remember, I said that I had full metal jacket and hollow points, I knew nothing about soft point bullets, which are the preferred bullet when it comes to most big game. When I shot the deer in the shoulder, the hollow point bullet did what it was designed to do, and that is to expand. Unfortunately, it expanded and broke apart before it could penetrate into the deer's vital organs. Use soft points, not hollow point bullets for deer hunting.

2. **Aim for behind the shoulder-** A behind the shoulder shot is preferred, not the shoulder itself; particularly when using a fast-

expanding bullet. Hollow points are not designed for deep penetration. Had I put the bullet behind the shoulder, I would have likely had better results and a shorter recovery.

3. **Wait a few minutes for the deer to die-** I learned that when you shoot a deer, give it time to die. When I shot the deer, I was hot on its trail within 30 seconds, only to find a pool of matted bloody pine straw where it had laid down. Had I given it time to die, it may would have bled out and died right there, 30 yards from where I shot it. But instead, I pushed that deer nearly a mile before I could get a finishing shot in it. If you don't see the deer go down, give it 20 minutes or so before you start tracking it. Deer and other animals have a tremendous will to survive, and they will fight to survive as long as there is breath in their lungs and blood in their veins. Give them time to die, and you won't have to look far for them.

Fulfilling the dream of a buffalo hunt

Hunting buffalo had been a life-long dream for me since childhood. While serving a tough combat tour in Ar Ramadi, Iraq in 2004, I promised myself that if I made it home alive, I was going to fulfill that dream. Instead of using a rifle like most hunters, I wanted to use a 12 ga. Remington 870 Express that I had named "Buster". When I told co-workers what I was planning, they thought that I was crazy! After all, buffalo are known for being tough to bring down and the shotgun has never been considered as a "big game" weapon, at least not at long range. The sheer size and mass of a buffalo makes people think of using a big caliber rifle. Most of the buffalo hunting websites that I visited had caliber requirements such as "magnum calibers only" or ".30-06 or higher". This initially presented me with a problem since I wanted to use a shotgun and slugs.

Shortly after arriving in Colorado Springs, Colorado, as I was browsing through the local swap-n-shop paper, I came across an ad stating that buffalo hunts were being booked for the months of November and December. This was the last place that I expected to see a buffalo hunting ad and initially I was skeptical, but after calling the number and inquiring about the hunt, I realized that this was the hunt that I had been looking for. The hunts were run by Jeff and Valerie Elem but unlike most other outfitters whose prices started at $1100, the Elems one day hunts started at a reasonable $750 for a 3-4 year old cow. I quickly booked a hunt and told them of my desire to take a buffalo with my shotgun.

Jeff told me that during his five years of guiding buffalo hunts, he has seen buffalo shot with everything from .25 calibers up to .458 Magnums - but never with a shotgun slug. I told the Elems of my theory that a big slow-moving slug performing better on buffalo than a "light" 180gr. bullet from a high-powered rifle. I believed that at 100 yards a slug would dump all of its energy inside the animal and stop, while the rifle bullet would likely punch through an animal, carrying much of its energy with it. The Elems agreed that this was an interesting theory and wanted to see how my slugs would perform on a buffalo, but warned me that buffalo are extremely tough animals! Jeff told me that of all the big game animals he has hunted throughout North America, buffalo were by far the toughest. I've actually seen video of a young bull being shot in the forehead with a .45-70 at 55 yards and it ran about 200 yards before allowing the hunter a second shot! Jeff told me story after story of seeing buffalo taking multiple shots before dropping. I told him that I did not think that I would have that problem if my theory proved to be true, but I'd bring along my .270 Winchester rifle just in case the buffalo were out of slug range.

    I had almost three weeks to prepare for the hunt and I must admit that I thought two or three times about buying a heavier caliber rifle and even looked at a .54 caliber muzzleloader. I finally put these ideas aside and focused on my slugs. The slug that I chose for this hunt was the 3" Brenneke Black Magic Magnum, a German made 600grain beast of a slug that produced over 3000 foot pounds of energy at the muzzle while traveling at 1575 feet per second. These slugs are actually recommended for "Big and Dangerous Game" by Brenneke. Most slug manufacturers do not advertise their slugs for such use. For years I have been a fan of Brenneke's slug because of their excellent accuracy through my smooth bore barrel and their unwillingness to deform upon impact. Ballistics on the box showed that at 100 yards these .73 caliber slugs produced 1200 foot pounds of energy. While most slug manufacturers recommend that you sight their slugs in at 50 yards, Brenneke recommends that you sight the Black Magic Magnum in at 88 yards, a distance that many would consider to be at the outer limits of a slugs' effective range. I expected my shot to be around 100 yards so I zeroed my scope in at 100 yards, and had no trouble putting the big slugs inside an 8 inch Shoot-N-C target at this distance. One rubbernecker at the range came over to take a look at my "sawed off shotgun" as he called it, and wanted to know if I was hitting anything out there. When I handed him binoculars to take a closer look, he replied. "I didn't know a slug would go that far!" Proof as to how much people underestimate the shotgun slug.

The morning of the hunt, as we hunters gathered around, it was not long before conversation started about firearm choices for the day. It was obvious that some people are more in to caliber size and name brand than their ability to shoot accurately. As expected, there were .30-06s, .300 Win Mags, .7mm Mags, and a .338 Mag. When I proudly told the group that I would be using a shotgun and slugs to shoot my buffalo, they laughed and looked at me like I was from Mars. Even when I told them that I was using 600 grain solid lead slugs, they still thought that I was a little weird. I told them that I had brought my .270 just in case the buffalo were out of shotgun range, but I was told that a .270 was also "too light" for buffalo. However, there was a guy there from California who was on my side, and said that my theory sounded good, and he actually wanted to see me do it. Hooray for Californians!

Arriving at the 9,000 acre ranch in Hartselle, Colorado the buffalo looked like little black dots at almost half a mile away. I grabbed Buster and a few slugs then grabbed the .270. After picking out a nice sized cow, Jeff coached the first hunter on making his shot. My rangefinder confirmed the range to be 189 yds. The hunter assumed a prone position and placed the crosshairs of his scope on the buffalo as I recorded the action through my video camera. He fired and I watched the bullet strike the 700-900 lb. buffalo right behind the shoulder. I was absolutely amazed at how the buffalo just flinched and kept walking as if nothing had happened. I asked what caliber was his rifle and he told me it was a .30-06. 15 minutes and 2 shots later, the cow was finally down for good. I was also in total disbelief when I saw a bull take two or three shots from a 7mm Magnum before finally going down. I remember taking one of the shotgun slugs out of my pocket and looking at the "little" 3-inch magnum and wondering if I was indeed crazy! Maybe I would have to use the .270 and 150 grain Nosler Partition bullets after all. I walked over to Jeff's wife who was watching the action from afar and told her that these buffalo were indeed tough to bring down. They were like tanks! Mike, a big burly mountain-man looking guy who had laughed at me earlier, offered to let me use his .338 Magnum. He said that he didn't mean to offend what I was shooting (my shotgun). I politely declined the use of his .338 and told him that I came to take a buffalo with a shotgun and that's exactly what I was going to do. No offense taken. Seeing a large bull take four shots before going down, lie there as if dead, then magically rise to its feet ,take two more shots before dropping, then rise one more time, lower his head and paw the ground in preparation to charge Jeff who had come to put the wounded beast out of his misery, made me wonder even more if a slug could get it done. A final shot to the neck from Jeff's rifle put the big bull down for good. By this point I was like the *Little Engine that Could*, "I think I can. I think I can." I told myself as I started to seriously question my own theory. Throughout all the shooting that had taken place so far, I was able to notice something. At ranges of 100 to 150 yards many of the bullets from the high-powered rifles were indeed punching holes through the buffalo and ricocheting off the ground on the other side. This part of my theory was true. This meant that the bullets were not dumping all of their energy inside the buffalo. Hopefully I would have better success with my bigger and slower -moving slugs.

    Several of us hopped into the back of a pickup truck to pursue the herd that had started running across the prairie. I was shocked to learn that the cow leading the herd had been shot at least once! A final shot dropped her, and as the herd settled down, Jeff was able to spot a big cow for me that stood a hump above the rest of the herd. I told Jeff that I was in no hurry and would wait all day in order to get within slug range. He asked me if we were close enough. I lased the herd with my rangefinder and the range was 123 yards. This was still within Buster's range but the problem was that I had never shot at this distance, and didn't know how the last 23 yards would affect the slug's trajectory. I opted to get a little closer. Jeff and I slowly walked towards the herd while eight onlookers watched from the bed of the pickup truck, waiting to witness the slugs' performance. Finding a bald spot on the ground some 85 to 90 yards away from the herd, I laid down on the ground, using my camera bag as a rest and hoped that the herd would not charge. The moment of truth was here. As I chambered a slug, Jeff made sure that I was seeing the same buffalo that he was seeing, then told me to shoot when ready. Concentrating like my life depended on it, I placed the crosshairs behind the cow's shoulder and squeezed the trigger. "Ba boom!" the shotgun announced its presence. I knew that I hit her but she didn't even move. I don't even think that she flinched. "Good shot!" Jeff hollered as he looked through his binoculars. Looking through my scope I saw that I could not have made a better shot. Right behind the shoulder was a large, almost quarter-sized hole. Knowing that this was a lethal shot and hoping to be the first one of the day to drop a buffalo with a single shot, I elected not to shoot again. Had we hopped on horses and chased the buffalo across the prairie like the Native Americans of yester year, the buffalo would have likely bled out and died sooner; but five minutes later she was showing no signs of dying. Taking aim, I fired another shot which landed 6 inches to the right of my first shot. Although I like to be able to say that she dropped on the second shot, the truth is that she did lie down, but as the herd started to move she stumbled to her feet, ready to move with the herd. I told Jeff that I couldn't believe that she was still standing after being hit in the vitals with 1,200 grains of lead. Jeff said that he didn't think that I was getting good penetration with the slugs and suggested that I aim

6 inches up from my last shot and shoot again. The third shot would put the slug high into the buffalo's lungs. Moving up to about 65 yards and placing the crosshairs a little higher, I squeezed the trigger again. This time there was a reaction. Upon the slug's impact, the buffalo jumped and mule kicked as blood shot out of her nose and mouth. Although I did not see it at the time due to the recoil, the third slug completely penetrated the buffalo and buried itself into the ground on the other side. Blood pumped from the entrance and exit holes as the buffalo made a short 30-yard trot, fell, coughed two times, and died. At last I had my buffalo and above all, - I did it with a shotgun and slugs!

To my knowledge, and anyone else's that I've talked to, I am the first person to have ever killed a buffalo with a shotgun slug. People don't usually think of a shotgun as a big game weapon, but I believe that there is nothing on the planet that cannot be killed with a shotgun slug. Slugs may not travel as fast or be as popular as the super-duper magnums on the market, but within their range they can definitely get the job done. Oddly enough, when I contacted the Colorado Department of Fish and Wildlife to ask about using shotgun slugs for elk hunting, I was told that I was not allowed to do so. I heard laughter in the background. Maybe they were laughing at something else, maybe they were laughing at my question. However, in 2005 the hunting regulations clearly stated that the minimum caliber for elk was .25 caliber. My slugs were .73 caliber. Perhaps they didn't think that it could be done because I later learned that there was nothing in the regulations that said I could not use a shotgun for hunting elk. At the meat processor I had the guys keep an eye out for two slugs that were believed to still be inside the buffalo. They indeed found two slugs and said that they were buried side by side just under the hide on the far side. So much for me not getting good penetration! Although I was not able to weigh the slugs, they deformed very little and appeared to have retained 100% of their weight. With 376 lbs. of boneless buffalo meat, I enjoyed buffalo for months.

This hunt is just one example of how powerful a shotgun slug truly is. Oh by the way, did you know that people in Alaska often carry shotguns loaded with Brenneke slugs for grizzly defense? After the buffalo hunt I retired my rifles and hunted the rest of the 2005-2006 season, and all of the 2006-2007 season with Buster. While I could have bought a brand-new rifle or a rifled barrel shotgun and used sabots, I wanted to show that it does not take sophistication to bring home the buffalo. It just takes a few well-placed shots. After all, the Native Americans did the same thing with homemade bows and arrows.

The 3 lessons learned from this hunt were:

1. **Never doubt yourself** – I believed that I could take a 900 plus pound animal with a smoothbore shotgun, and I did. While a lot of people didn't think that I knew what I was talking about when I told them of my plans, it turned out that **they** didn't know what **they** were talking about because a quality 12 ga slug such as the Brenneke Black Magic Magnum is absolutely deadly on big and dangerous game.

2. **Don't get caught up in the high-powered rifle debate**- Some people can spend hours debating over caliber size, effectiveness, and ballistic coefficiency, but none of that matters at close range. A well-placed bullet to the vitals from almost any caliber will get the job done.

3. **Keep it simple**- A pump action shotgun is about as simple as it gets when it comes to big game hunting. It all boils down to having faith in your ability to make a clean shot, and putting time in at the range to learn you and your firearm's capabilities. Oftentimes, our guns are capable of shooting much better than we are. It's not always about name brand, caliber size, or what's the newest craze on the market.

Author's 900 lb buffalo taken with a 12ga shotgun and slugs

An Oklahoma Deer Hunt

Offering both whitetail and mule deer, turkey, small game, waterfowl, and a host of other game, Oklahoma is easily one of my favorite states to hunt. The terrain in the western part of the state is easily comparable to Kansas. Although I got my earliest experiences in hunting in the small town of Talladega AL, it is Oklahoma where I shot my first turkey and cut my teeth on deer hunting.

In 2006 I lucked into a hunting lease and had the privilege of hunting a sizeable chunk of land in the far corner of Western Oklahoma, about 45 minutes from the little town of Buffalo, Oklahoma. During this time I was just getting into bow hunting but I had been into archery since the 5th grade. I was also just getting into treestands and while I was comfortable with a ladder stand, the last thing that I wanted any part of, was a climbing treestand. Sure, they give the hunter a tremendous advantage by getting the hunter's scent above the deer and allowing for greater visibility, but the idea of getting into a contraption and climbing 25 feet up a tree and hanging there, did not seem like fun or smart to me at the time. I had jumped out of airplanes 43 times while being assigned to the 82nd Airborne Division but using a climbing treestand seemed crazy! So when the 2006 bow season came in, I chose to hunt by sitting on a camp stool in waist high grass about 25 yards from the feeder. We knew that the deer were coming to the feeder just before sunset and some of the guys had pictures of nice bucks that were coming through the area. I had positioned my stool to give me a clear shot at any deer that came to the feeder. All I had to do was ease into a seated shooting position, take aim, and send an arrow right over the high grass into my target.

Sitting there in my leaf suit, I had roughly two hours before sunset and I was doing my best to sit still. I would peek over the grass looking around for any sign of a deer, but saw nothing. I don't care how old you are, sitting still can be a challenge, especially when you are uncomfortable. The stool I was sitting on did not have a back rest. So I squirmed, shuffled my feet, and fanned away the flies and gnats that were pestering me. I had not shot a deer with a bow at this point and I was hoping that today would be my day. It seemed like an eternity and although the sun was starting to set, I still had not seen a deer. Convinced that I would not see anything, and partially motivated by boredom, I un-nocked my arrow and stood up, only to see that a big bodied 8-point buck was about 10 yards from the feeder! It was the biggest buck that I had ever seen while hunting. Hidden from view by the grass, I had no idea the buck was there, and he had no idea I was there either, until I stood up. When the buck saw me he bolted across the prairie as I fumbled to nock an arrow.

"Please come back. Please come back." I told myself. Inexperience told me to sit back down, act like nothing had happened, and hope that he would be dumb enough to come back to the feeder, but that was not going to happen. I had been busted, and that deer was long gone.

I guess that you can say I felt a combination of excitement and frustration; excited because I had been that close to getting a shot at a deer with my bow, but frustrated because had I just stayed a little longer, I would have gotten a shot at a nice 8 pointer. That's hunting though, and when you're just starting out, you learn things the hard way. You make mistakes, but those mistakes will make you a better hunter in the long run.

The 3 things that I learned from this hunt were:

1. Stay put until the last second of legal shooting light!- Had I just stayed put for another 60 seconds I would have had a shot at the deer, from the ground, at about 25 yards.

2. Get comfortable- When you're comfortable you move less and are more likely to stay put. With no back support on my stool I was squirming like a kid in time out.

3. Look before you move- It pays to move slowly, slower than a sloth, and to look around before you just pop up like a Jack in the Box. Looking back, if I had eased up off my stool and looked around, I would have seen the deer walking towards me.

Kansas duck hunt with a 5-month-old Chesapeake Bay Retriever

Although I don't do it as much as I would like to, duck hunting is my favorite type of hunting. There's just something about watching the sunrise and hearing the whistling of wings flapping overhead and watching the dog work. There are not many more majestic sights than to see a flock of ducks cupped up with outstretched feet, getting ready to land into your decoys. Add a good retriever to the mix and it is heaven on Earth.

Although I have been hunting for most of my life, I was a late bloomer when it came to duck hunting. I did not get my first introduction until 2010 while being stationed at Ft. Leavenworth, Kansas. The Army had sent me there for Intermediate Leadership Education, a course that used to be called CGSC, or Command and General Staff College. Being the hunter that I am, my first stop was to the Leavenworth Rod and Gun Club on base, as I wanted to be sure that I learned the requirements needed for me to hunt there. It is always fun joining and interacting with the members of the Rod and Gun club, or Sportsman clubs, when being assigned to new military bases. There is often a variety of game available to hunt and plenty of fellow hunters to connect with. Although I had hunted seven other military bases in the past such as Ft. Bragg, NC, Ft. Gordon, GA, Ft. Jackson, SC, Ft. Gillem, GA, Ft. Benning, GA, Ft. Hood, TX, and

Ft. Carson, CO, this was my first time being stationed in the Midwest, and it was during this time at Ft. Leavenworth that I met guys from the local Ft. Leavenworth Ducks Unlimited Chapter. Ducks Unlimited is one of America's premier waterfowl hunting and conservation organizations with hundreds of chapters across the country.

It was here at Ft. Leavenworth, and through the Ducks Unlimited Chapter that I received my first introduction to waterfowl hunting, at the ripe age of 39. Veteran duck hunters such as Mike Swanson, Jeff Irvine, and Steve Hammock were instrumental in teaching me the ins and outs of hunting ducks, snow geese, Canadian geese, and speckle belly geese. Over the months that I was at Leavenworth, I went on as many duck hunts as I could. I figured that I would have plenty of time to hunt deer after I left Kansas. Afterall, the South is not known as a duck hunting destination. On one of these hunts I got an introduction to the Chesapeake Bay Retriever. The Chesapeake Bay Retriever is a large breed of hunting dog, created for retrieving ducks out of the Chesapeake Bay's ice cold waters. Like most people, I had never seen a Chessie as they are sometimes called. I thought it was a Chocolate Lab. I could not help but notice how impervious the Chessie was to the freezing cold water, and how readily it took to the cold water to retrieve ducks. Now everybody has their preference when it comes to duck dogs, with most people seeming to prefer a Labrador Retriever. After all, Labs were once the most popular dog in America until the French Bull Dog came along and took the title. I remembered that Mike preferred the Chessie and Jeff preferred the Labrador.

Fast forward three years, and I was the proud owner of a 5-month old Chesapeake Bay Retriever that I named "Razor", and was back at Leavenworth for another assignment. I got reacquainted with the Ducks Unlimited Committee and two months later, we were on our annual committee hunt for opening day of the 2014 duck season. The location we hunted was Jamestown Wildlife Management Area. Since I was still somewhat new to duck hunting, I figured that I would tag along with the rest of the crew and hunt in a group like we did in past years, but instead, I was surprised that I would have to hunt by myself. While I had planned to tag along with Jeff, he was concerned that my dog would get his dog pregnant. Jeff had a champion British Lab, a female, and she was in heat. He did not want to take any chances of my dog mating with his. I explained to Jeff that Razor was only 5 months old, a puppy. Sure, he was the same size as Jeff's Lab, 50lbs, but Jeff's dog was 5 or 6 years old and Razor was only 5 months old. He still had his puppy teeth in. The last thing on Razor's mind was mating. Not wanting to debate the issue, I agreed to hunt alone. This would be my first time hunting ducks alone, and with my own dog. Driving across the WMA I found a nice marsh that had skinny water, or shallow water as it's also known. This was prime teal habitat since teal are more likely to land in shallow water compared to mallards and other big ducks. Finding a nice spot along the marsh, I figured that since there wasn't much cover, I'd make a little blind by sticking branches in front of us. But being a puppy, and having a love for chewing on sticks, Razor would gnaw on the branches and pull them out of the ground as fast as I could put them in the ground. The ducks did not disappoint as teal swooped by like little fighter jets. I'll be honest. I took several shots, multiple shots, but missed every time. It can be tough sometimes hitting ducks, especially teal. After a couple of hours of missing, and seeing teal come by in flocks, singles, and pairs, Razor's attention span was fading fast. He was more interested in chewing up the blind than watching for ducks. After a while, a lone teal flew in front of me at about 30 yards. I swung the shotgun, pulled the trigger, and the teal dropped and bounced across the water, like how someone skips a rock across the water. I was happy that I had finally hit a duck because I would soon be out of shells. Razor had grown so accustomed to me missing and had been hearing gunshots all morning, that he had not realized I had actually hit a duck.

"Go get him Raze!" I told him, hoping that he would go retrieve the duck. Instead, Razor looked at me like I was trying to teach him Arabic.

"Go get it Raze!" I told him again.

Razor stood up, wagging his tail, not having a clue as to what I was talking about. Looking back, he really did not know what I was talking about. When I shot the duck, he was preoccupied chewing on a stick and never saw the duck hit the water. So to get his attention, I threw a rock out towards the duck. Razor took off looking like a little fat grizzly cub bounding through the water to where the rock landed. When he got to the duck, I was hoping that he would pick it up and bring it back, so that I could say that he retrieved his first duck at 5 months old. But instead, once Razor got out to where the rock splashed, he noticed the duck floating and immediately started barking at it.

"Come on Raze, pick up the duck" I mumbled to myself.

But again, he barked and pawed at it. After a couple minutes of watching him bark and paw, I realized that it just was not going to happen. He was not going to retrieve it. So, I walked out to get the duck myself. As I reached down to grab the duck, Razor gently bit the ducks' wing and pulled it away from me.

"Get it Raze, get it!" I encouraged him.

Razor proceeded with the barking and pawing, and when I reached down a second time to get the duck, Razor grabbed the duck and pulled it away and drug it all the way back to the bank!

"Good job Raze, good job!" I told him, proud as I could be that he had just retrieved his first duck, a blue winged teal, at the young age of 5 months old. I took a second to snap a picture of Razor and the duck, as he dropped it at the bank, then picked it up again, holding it gently by the neck. Yes! Razor had retrieved his first duck, at just 5 months old!

When we met up with the other hunters after the hunt, I could not wait to tell the guys about Razors' first retrieve. They were impressed, but the next morning, Razor and I still had to hunt alone. But that was okay, I had shot at, and missed, enough ducks to feel like I knew what I was doing now. Razor had retrieved a duck, so we were good. We spent most of the morning driving around looking for marshes to hunt, checking out Buffalo Marsh, Greenwing Marsh, and a few others. We had lunch and decided on hunting a marsh that happened to have no other hunters on it. As we walked down the trail to the desolate marsh, I noticed that there were ducks in the area. I also noticed a nice sized pond that looked like a good place to set up and to throw out my decoys. While I had walked through marsh water on the previous days' hunt, this pond looked deep. The last thing I wanted to do was to start walking through it, drop into deep water, and have my waders fill with water, causing me to drown. So I walked along the banks of the marsh and found a nice spot to set up. I threw the decoys out, mainly teal and mallard decoys, and settled in for the hunt. As I looked up, I could see that the sky was literally a waterfowl highway. There were ducks flying in the distance in multiple directions, a huge flock of geese flying to the right 200 feet up, another flock of 30-40 geese flying to the left perhaps 400 feet up, and 50 or so ducks flying over the trees out in the distance. Occasionally ducks would swoop overhead and I'd shoot, and miss. Then the action seemed to just stop. Legal shooting hours ended at sunset and I had a couple of hours left to see what would happen. I figured that the ducks would definitely be moving just before sunset as they moved from their feeding areas back to their loafing areas, and like clockwork, I started seeing low-flying ducks coming in overhead. It just so happened that the ducks were coming from behind me, which worked out perfectly. You see, as the ducks would fly overhead, they would be within easy shotgun range before they realized Razor and I were there. Again, if you didn't know, teal are some fast-flying ducks! As a small flock of blue wing teal approached, I turned around, lined the bead up with a duck, and pulled the trigger. "Boom!!" Got 'em! I told myself as the teal folded up and landed onto the water 20 yards away. I thought about walking out to the duck but just did not feel comfortable not knowing how deep the pond was. However, I had a hunting partner that was made for moments like this; Razor, my trusty Chesapeake Bay Retriever. Again, this breed is one of the best duck retrievers and water dogs known to man. Their paws are webbed, and their coat is pretty much water repellent. They are duck retrieving machines!

"Go get him Razor!" I told the young pup.

This time Razor needed no encouragement. He had seen the duck fall onto the water, and at my command, he charged into the water headed for the duck. Reaching the duck, he quickly grabbed it and swam back to shore. Before I could take the duck from his mouth, another flock of teal came in. This time they were to my right at a distance of 30 yards. I picked out a duck, swung the shotgun past it, and pulled the trigger. "Boom!" the duck folded up and dropped into the water. This time, Razor did not wait for my command, he took to the water like a moth to a flame, and retrieved the duck like he had been doing this for years! You see, there is a thing called instinct, and as a retriever, bred for retrieving ducks, Razor's natural instinct was kicking in. More ducks came in and the results were the same as the first two ducks. It was as if the stars and planets had aligned for me, I was shooting like a pro, not missing a single bird. The most impressive retrieve of the day was when one duck was wounded and managed to swim to the far side of the pond. It had to be 40 or 50 yards. Razor swam to the other side of the pond to retrieve the duck. When it was all said and done, I had six ducks on the bank, all retrieved by Razor, my five-month-old puppy!

I gotta admit it, I was feeling pretty proud of my Razor. A lot of you hunting dog owners know this feeling. While I had started the hunt expecting to hunt with more seasoned duck hunters and more experienced retrievers, it turns out that Razor and I did just fine by ourselves. Retrieving 7 ducks on his first duck hunt at just 5 months old? Yep, I'll take that all day long. As folks used to say where I'm from, "This dog will hunt!"

The three lessons learned from this hunt were:

1. **Shoot sporting clays and skeet-** Hitting a moving target with a shotgun can be challenging. Shooting several rounds of sporting clays and skeet would have help me not waste so many shells on my first day of the hunt.

2. **Don't be afraid to hunt your puppy-** I had been training and working with Razor since he was 10 weeks old. He was already retrieving by then and I had taught him to be steady to gunfire. The best way to train your puppy is by on-the-job training. Sometimes the best on-the-job training is an actual hunt.

3. **Have fun!-** For those of you that hunt with your dogs, it is amazing how much fun you can have with a dog on a hunt. It is just something about watching a dog do its thing, whether it be a bird dog, squirrel dog, rabbit dog, or duck dog.

Keep hunting y'all!

Razor's first duck retrieve at 5 months old

Razor with a limit of ducks on Day 2

Oklahoma Muzzleloader deer hunt

Muzzleloaders, also known as black powder rifles, can be a fun and primitive way to hunt both big and small game. I had heard of muzzleloaders, and seen a few on store shelves over the past 25 years, but never felt the need to buy one. Afterall, the one or two deer that I had killed up until this point, had all been killed with a regular modern-day rifle. Well, upon returning from Iraq in 2005 I found myself stationed in Oklahoma for recruiting duty. I met a local mechanic that lived to do three things- work on cars, fish, and hunt! While leaning over the hood of my Plymouth Duster one day, the mechanic, whose name was John, asked me if I knew of anybody that would be interested in joining their hunting lease in Western Oklahoma, not too far from Kansas. The price was $650 a year per person, and the lease was about 7 square miles, consisting of small game, turkey, whitetail deer, and the occasional mule deer. I jumped at the opportunity and as a new hunter, found myself in the company of two guys that had been hunting for as long as I had been alive.

In case you didn't know, there are hunting seasons, which means that there are times of the year, and specific dates that you can hunt certain animals. Usually, archery season comes in first, followed by muzzleloader season, then followed by regular rifle season. Muzzleloader season is also known as "primitive weapon" season, and it wasn't long before John was asking me if I was ready.

"Nope. I don't even have a muzzleloader. But I can buy one." I told John.

"I have one that I'll sell you for a good price. It's an older Knight" he replied, referring to the brand of the gun.

I bought the gun, and after a lesson of how to load and shoot it, I was ready for the hunt that was coming up in two weeks. Due to work, and the fact that the lease was a four-hour drive from my house, I only hunted on weekends and holidays.

On the day of the hunt, we arrived at one of the many wheat fields that were scattered across the landscape. It was quite a difference hunting in Western Oklahoma compared to hunting in Alabama, where I grew up. Whereas you can't go two steps without seeing a tree in Alabama. Trees were scarce in the plains of western Oklahoma. A lot of scrub brush and a few cottonwood trees, but nothing a timber company would want to harvest. However, John carried me to one of the few trees that was in the area and there, about 14 feet off the ground, was a treestand secured by ratchet straps to a tree that was about as fat as a dinner plate.

"Wait, you want me to sit in that?!" I asked him, figuring there's no way I was going up there.

"Yeah, it'll hold you. You and I are about the same size and it holds me just fine. You gotta sit real still though because if you're moving, the deer are going to see you when they come in." John told me.

Not wanting to appear overly concerned, code word for "terrified", I said "Okay no problem", and proceeded to climb up the tree using the climbing sticks that were also ratchet strapped to the tree. I consider myself to be fearless, but back at that time, that skinny tree scared me to death! Getting situated in the stand, I pulled my rifle up into the tree with me, pulled the plunger back and waited. Yes, it was an older style muzzleloader that utilized the plunger type cocking system where you would cock the hammer so to speak, by pulling a spring-loaded plunger back until it locks, then you pull the trigger to release the bolt which strikes the primer, causing the gun to fire. In 2005, it was a high-tech advancement compared to the flash pan and flint methods of the 1700's. However, the plunger style muzzleloaders are definitely outdated by today's standard.

This would be an evening hunt, and I was excited to see what would come by, as it would still be a couple of hours before the sun set. I was taking it all in, the chirping of the birds, the high pitch call of a red tail hawk flying overhead, and the sounds of the gentle breeze. After about an hour and a half of sitting, I looked over to see two does walking towards my direction. I tightened my grip on the muzzleloader, hoping that they would continue walking towards my stand, and the corn that was sprinkled nearby. I cocked the plunger when the deer got within 50 yards. They continued walking to 25 yards of me, then to 10 yards, as they continued to the corn that was scattered behind me and to my left. Most folks would have shot as soon as they saw the deer, but I wanted to see if more, particularly bucks, were following. As they munched on corn, I realized that they were alone and decided to take a shot at the biggest of the does. She was quartering away from me with her head down and the wind was blowing my scent away from them. They had no idea I was there. I rotated my body to the left, lined my sights on the does ribs and pulled the trigger. Ba -boom!! The muzzleloader barked as smoke billowed from the barrel. Luckily the wind was blowing in my direction which blew the smoke away from the deer, allowing me to see what was happening. As the bullet entered behind the does' last rib and plowed through her chest, she stiffened up with her legs locked, appearing to freeze in place momentarily. She stood in that pose for a split second before turning and running full speed out into the wheat field, before collapsing. I looked back at the smaller doe to see that she was standing motionless, her eyes and ears locked on the bigger doe. As the bigger doe lay dead out in the field, the smaller one trotted out to the dead deer. I was a fairly new hunter at this time and as the smaller deer trotted, it dawned on me that the smaller deer was actually a fawn.

"Oh no." I thought. Now let me tell you a little secret about myself. At the age of 4 or 5, I went to see the movie *Bambi,* and I vividly remember crying my eyeballs out when the hunter shot Bambis' mama. I had just shot Bambi's mama!!?? Man I felt so bad. As I walked out to the field the fawn didn't run. I was 50 yards from it and it still didn't run. I felt bad, real bad, and for a moment, I thought about shooting the fawn too, but I decided to let it live and hoped that another doe would adopt it.

As I field dressed the doe I learned what a "wet doe" was, another reminder that she was with a fawn. What is a "wet doe"? Well, a wet doe is one that still has milk in her mammary glands. I learned this as I was cutting around her tits and had the white milk seep out and mix in with the blood. Yeah, it's gross, it's unfortunate, but when you're new to hunting and only see deer as big deer and small deer, these things happen. I wasn't proud of it but hey, this hunt taught me several lessons.

The three lessons learned were:

1. **Muzzleloaders work just fine for hunting-** Muzzleloaders are just as capable of killing deer as a modern centerfire rifle. You'll be limited to 100-200 yards, but most deer in America are killed at 100 yards or less.

2. **Study your prey-** It pays to spend time in the woods learning what fawns look like and deer behavior. Being a new hunter and this being the second or third deer that I had shot, I didn't know it was a mother and fawn. Remember, back in the memory of my first

hunt, I shot a fawn, a little button buck, thinking it was a mature deer. With this hunt, I learned the importance of knowing what a fawn looks like and what a mature doe looks like; because I did not like the fact that I shot Bambi's mama!

3. **Tree size does not always matter-** While I was terrified that the tree would break or not be able to hold me, I learned that the dinner-sized plate thickness of the tree was more than enough to hold my weight. Being new to tree stands, I wanted to be in something like a big hickory or oak tree. Size does not always matter.

Ft. Benning hog and deer drive

Located in Southwest Georgia along the banks of the Chattahoochee River lies Ft. Benning, a 182,000 acre U.S Army installation that is prime habitat for hunting deer and wild hogs. Ft. Benning has now been renamed Ft. Moore but back in 2009 I received an invitation to participate in a pig hunt from a fellow co-worker. I was in the Army, stationed at Ft. McPherson, which is now the home of Tyler Perry Studios. The hunting party would be made up primarily of active duty and retired Soldiers, with a few civilian guests sprinkled in.

Being a gun guy, I had multiple options of guns to use, but I settled on taking a Winchester model 1894 lever action, chambered in .44 Magnum. With a magazine capacity of 10 rounds, and the power to kill any animal in North America, I felt well-armed for the hunt. Speaking of the hunt, the plan was to do man-drives where one group of hunters, the "standers", would be positioned throughout the woods while another group of hunters, the "drivers", would start about half a mile away, hooping and hollering while walking in the direction of the standers. For those combat arms Soldiers out there, you may call this a "movement to contact". What you are doing is driving or pushing the animals towards the standers. If it is a good drive, you will hear gunshots as you approached the other hunters. Sometimes a quarter of a mile away, and again as you walk the last 300 yards. It is common for a hunting party to end up with 5 or 6 harvested animals upon the completion of one good drive.

Being that this was my first time doing this type of hunt, and because I saw the possibility for something to go wrong, like somebody accidentally getting shot, I decided to bring my climbing treestand and get about 15 feet off of the ground. That way, whenever the shooting started, I'd be well out of harms way. I would learn later that the treestand isn't really needed if you have a group of seasoned deer drive hunters.

On the morning of our first hunt, I was one of the standers. I was dropped off alongside the road and told to go into the woods about 200 yards and find a good spot. The truck proceeded about two hundred yards down the road and another stander was told to do the same thing. Finding a good tall tree, I attached my stand and ascended to a height of 15 feet. From where I was perched, I could see all around me and had good fields of fire. Meaning that I had plenty of room to shoot. After sitting for 30 minutes or so, I could hear the faint sounds of the drivers hollering, and making noise to move the animals.

"Alright, I hope I see something come my way" I told myself as I scanned the woods looking for hogs and deer. A few minutes later I caught a glimpse of tan. It was two does trotting through the underbrush trying to evade the drivers. As the deer passed within 40 yards of my treestand, I took aim at the lead doe, and squeezed the trigger. "Booooom!!!" the .44 barked and the deer collapsed and did not move. I quickly worked the lever and swung to the smaller doe that had stopped in its tracks after the first doe was shot. "Booom!!" the .44 Magnum barked again with the sound echoing through the woods. The second deer dropped in its tracks as well.

"Wow! These handloads work really well! "referring to the custom handloaded ammunition that I was using.

You see, about four years earlier, after I returned from Iraq in 2005, I met a guy in rural Colorado that introduced me to reloading. I wanted a load that would also work for elk, so he found a recipe that utilized a 210grain jacketed hollow point Speer bullet and 25 grains of Winchester 296 gun powder. I loaded up 50 rounds using this recipe. I never chronographed the load to see how fast it was moving, or tested the pound feet of energy, but it was dropping deer as if the ground had been snatched from underneath them. Looking back, I would not have used that bullet on an elk as I would opt for a cast core or soft point bullet. Something that would give me deeper penetration.

As the drivers passed by, I indicated to one of them, Bob, a retired Special Forces guy, that I had shot two deer. He asked where were they, and I pointed over to where they were, as I climbed down from the tree. Without me asking, he walked over, found the deer, and started dragging it to the road. I grabbed the other and did the same. Taking a closer look at the deer, there was only one hole in the deer, right behind the shoulders, as the bullets had not passed through. Upon gutting the deer and quartering it, the autopsy was shocking! While the bullets had not passed through, they had fragmented, basically exploding inside the deer. It literally looked as if a small grenade had gone off, creating massive organ and tissue damage. Now, I know that some hunters prefer that a bullet penetrates an animal and exit. It leaves a good blood trail which is handy for tracking. However, some of us hunters prefer a bullet and load that will dump all of its energy inside an animal WITHOUT exiting. When this happens, no tracking is required because the animal often drops in its tracks. What happens when you dump 1500 pounds of energy inside a 140-pound animal? They rarely take a step and if they do, they don't step very far. I was indeed pleased with the bullets' performance and the fact that I had two deer on the first hunt, and the hunt was just getting started.

Over the course of the next few hours, I took turns being both stander and driver. The terrain at Ft. Benning can be downright nasty at times. Sure, there are plenty of long leaf pine trees and open areas, but other areas are swampy, full of briars, and thick with snakes. I'll get to one of those stories in a future *Memory of the Hunt*, but I crossed my fair share of knee-high creeks that day. During the evening of day one I found myself being a stander again. This time I decided to leave the climbing treestand on the truck, and took a small folding stool to sit on, as I would be hunting from the ground. The area I was told to go to, did not look promising. As I remember, I was sitting on a small bank, with open woods behind me and a thick brushy area in front of me.

"Oh well, this is the direction the drivers will be coming, so hopefully they will push something my way." I told myself as I just knew that I was in a bad spot.

After 20 minutes or so of sitting, I caught movement of something over my left shoulder. I slowly turned my head to see a doe at about 35 yards, high stepping towards my direction. She must have caught my sent or knew that something was up. I eased the rifle around the tree, but she saw me and started running at a slow trot towards the thicket. I swung the gun towards the deer, putting the front sight just in front of her shoulder and pulled the trigger. "Booom!!!" the .44 barked and found its mark, high in the deer's' shoulder. It looked as if the bullet hit her in mid stride because upon impact, the doe did a summersault and landed headfirst into the thicket! She kicked around for a bit then laid still. It was only 20 minutes into the drive and the funny thing about it was that I had not heard the first hoop from the drivers. They were still half a mile away. Needless to say, I was pumped and on cloud nine as to how the hunt was going.

After the hunt we cleaned and quartered our deer, I think four or five were shot that evening. Two or three hogs were shot as well. The meat was divided among the hunters. That was the rule so that everyone went home with meat, regardless of whether you shot anything or not. The only way you went home empty handed is if you did not want any. We later cooked meals, had drinks, and prepared for the second day of the hunt.

The next morning I found myself being a stander again. This time too, I took my stool instead of the tree stand. The stool was light and easy to carry while the treestand, although aluminum, was large and cumbersome, and took too long for me to get into the tree versus just sitting down behind one. This particular spot looked promising. It was semi-open, well secluded, and allowed me to see out to about 80 yards. After a while, I saw a doe feeding towards me. It was the biggest doe that I had seen on the hunt, a nice fat one with a long nose and grey face. The wind was in my face, which was perfect. She had no idea that I was there. Eventually she got to within 50 yards of me and was quartering away. I put the front sight on her shoulder and pulled the trigger. "Boooom!!" at the sound of the shot the doe jumped into the air and ran off in the direction that she had come.

"Oh yes, I got another one!" I told myself as I worked the lever to chamber another round.

After giving the deer time to lay down and die, I got up from my stool and went to the spot where she was standing when I shot her. I saw blood, deep red blood. I felt that it was a good shot, but as I searched around for the deer, I could not find her. The blood trail got fainter and fainter until I eventually lost the trail. Where could she be? Three other deer had met a quick death when hit by the .44 Magnum, but this doe was gone! "Rich", one of the drivers had come along and asked if I got anything. I told him that I had shot another doe. I took him to the spot where the blood trail started and after searching, neither he or I could find the deer.

"Maybe you grazed her. Come on let's go, we gotta get back to the trucks." Rich told me.

As I walked to the truck I was puzzled as what could have gone wrong. I obviously hit her. But as I replayed the shot over in my head, I realized that I likely had not hit the deer's vitals, but had done significant damage to her shoulder. Not what any hunter wants, but unfortunately it happens sometimes. Perhaps if I was using a jacketed soft point bullet, it would have done more damage. Perhaps broken the shoulder bone, or penetrated through into the neck. I guess that I'll never know.

Looking back at the memories of this hunt, I was pretty proud of myself. Here I was on a deer drive with fellow Soldiers, and a few good 'ol country folks, using a traditional lever action rifle with open sights, and shooting four deer. Most all the other guys were using scopes. Yes, it is unfortunate that I made a bad shot on the big doe but again, it happens sometimes. The coyotes and buzzards were surely grateful for an easy meal.

The three lessons that I learned from this hunt were:

1: **Using a climbing tree stand made sense** as it greatly reduces fratricide, which is, shooting your fellow hunters by accident. I think that I was the first person in their group to do that. In all deer drives after that, they required standers to bring climbing tree stands.

2. **Teamwork makes the dream work.** I had heard of the term "hunting party", but this was my first time seeing one in action and seeing the sharing of the harvest among hunters. In some of the past group hunts I had been on, it was every man for himself.

3. **I should have waited for the big doe to give me a broadside shot.** While my handloaded ammunition worked like a charm on broadside shots, it was not the best choice for a shoulder shot. Although I was happy with how the bullet exploded inside the deers vitals, I was not pleased with how it may have exploded on the doe's shoulder and prevented penetration. I'll choose my shots more carefully next time and continue to put meat in the freezer.

Keep hunting y'all!

Author and two does taken with his .44 Magnum rifle

Hunting the Kansas Rut

One great memory of the hunt comes from Kansas, during the 2010 deer rut. I had been assigned to Ft. Leavenworth and had joined the Ft. Leavenworth Rod and Gun Club. Most military installations have some type of Sportsman Club where hunters and fishermen alike can come together and enjoy hunting and fishing along with other types of outdoor recreation. For all of you servicemembers and retirees out there, I highly suggest that you join your installations' Sportsmen or Rod and Gun Club. You'll meet great people and find opportunities to participate in all sorts of hunts and outdoor activities.

Being that I was on the committee of the Leavenworth Rod and Gun Club, part of my volunteer duties required me to work the check-in station Saturday and Sunday mornings. Not all Saturdays and Sundays, just one or two whenever time permitted. My duties were to sign hunters in for the hunt and to assist with getting biometrics on the deer that hunters brought in. Prior to the rut I had scouted several areas around the base and had seen good deer sign in several areas, but particularly behind the skeet range. Now, one thing I have learned over my years of hunting is that you can use common sounds, such as trains, airplanes, heavy machinery, road traffic, and yes, gun ranges, to mask your hunting presence; particularly gun shots. So, my plan for opening day was to hunt behind the skeet range. The logic was simple. First, there were good signs of deer in the area. Second, for all their lives, these deer had been hearing gunshots. from noon or so, all the way to seven or eight o'clock at night. Third, few hunters considered hunting behind the skeet range because they figured that the noise would scare off the deer. Not me, I knew something they didn't know. But, for the early morning of this particular Saturday, I was manning the check station. Several hunters came in to sign out for the morning hunt and to mark the area where they would be hunting. Later in the morning a few hunters returned with their harvest. All along I was waiting for my shift to end, eager to get into the woods myself. If I'm not mistaken, my shift was from 6am to 10am.

      Time passed, and before I knew it, it was 10 o'clock. A few hunters had come in with a doe or a couple of nice bucks, and as soon as my relief showed up, I peeled out of the parking lot like I was rushing to a fire. But, instead of heading to the woods, I headed to the post office. I had to mail an important package. Looking at my watch, I figured that it would be 10:30 by the time I got to my hunting spot. 10:30am was a whole lot later than I had planned to be in the woods, but since it was the rut, I knew that deer would be moving all day. Arriving at my hunting spot, I parked my truck and lugged my climbing stand 300 yards or so to the spot I planned to hunt. I was hunting with a 12 ga pump shotgun and had it loaded with Brenneke K.O slugs. There are dozens of options out there when it comes to shotgun slugs, but in my opinion, Brenneke makes some of the best slugs on the market. The German company was created in the late 1800's and their slugs are still highly regarded to this day. Reaching my spot, I attached my stand to the tree and propped my shotgun against another tree. My plan was to use some bottled doe urine as an attractant and pour some on cotton balls that I was placing about waist high on limbs and branches around my stand. This is one technique that can be successful during the rut, as the wind will carry the scent of the doe urine through the woods and hopefully bring bucks to you. I was placing urine-soaked cotton balls about 15 yards from my tree when all of a sudden, I heard something crashing through the woods towards me and I heard "burp-burp-burp". I figured it was a deer coming my way but I could not identify the "Burp" sound. I turned my head to see a doe running towards me, with a big 10-pointer hot on her trail grunting, that is what the "Burp" sound was. It was a tending grunt, the sound a buck makes when it is on the trail of a doe that is in heat. Behind the 10-pointer was a 6-pointer, and behind the 6-pointer was a spike, all chasing that one doe.

"Ahh man!" I told myself, realizing that I was caught totally off guard.

The doe ran past me and stopped 10 yards away. When the doe stopped, the big 10 pointer stopped about 5 yards behind her, and the others did as well.

"Uh oh." I told myself as I stood there with a cotton ball in one hand, and an open bottle of doe pee in the other. The moment may have lasted for five or six seconds but it seemed like a lot longer. In this time my life flashed before my eyes, as I thought of how this could end really bad. Here I was, standing in between a rutting buck with steam coming out of his nostrils, and a doe in estrous. His massive rack had antlers that could do serious damage to me if he decided to attack. I thought back to stories I've heard of hunters getting attacked by bucks because they put doe pee on their clothes, and here I was holding an open bottle of doe in estrous pee, meaning that it was collected from a doe while she was in heat, meaning that she was ready to mate. I wasn't comfortable with the fact that I was standing between the buck and his doe, and I *definitely* did not want to get sexually assaulted by a buck. I glanced over at my shotgun leaning against the tree and for a second, I thought about making a run for it, but instead I just stayed perfectly still. Suddenly, the doe sprinted off causing the bucks to pick up the chase once again. I let out a sigh of relief, finished placing my cotton balls, and climbed up the tree.

Reaching a height of about 20 feet, I pulled my shotgun into the stand with me and prayed that the deer would come back. It was a beautiful day, temperature in the mid 40's and leaves falling peacefully to the ground. It was not long before the shooting started up at the skeet range. I sat there in the tree, swaying in the wind with birdshot from the range occasionally falling down through the trees, sounding like light rainfall. About 20 minutes later, I heard the familiar sounds of deer running towards my direction. I strained my neck looking through the trees to see another doe running, and a buck in pursuit. It was like an exact repeat of what I had seen earlier. I was seeing everything from the side, and when I saw the buck, he looked good to me, with antlers that swept up and out towards his nose. The doe ran past me at 20 yards then stopped. She must have caught my scent! Upon seeing that the doe had stopped, the buck stopped too. This time I was ready. I took aim behind the buck's shoulder and squeezed the trigger. "Booooom!" The slug found it's mark, and the buck collapsed in its tracks, letting out a long grunt. "Buuuuuuurrrp" I chambered another shell and looked to see where the doe was. She was still standing there, but looking back at the buck to see what just happened. See, it pays to hunt in an area where the animals are used to hearing gunfire. She didn't move, even after I had fired a 12 ga shotgun just 15 yards from her. Maybe she was deaf. Maybe she was unphased by gunshots. I don't know, but she was standing behind a tree with her head and neck exposed. Her shoulder and vitals were completely shielded by the tree. I swung the shotgun to my left, lined up the sights on her neck and pulled the trigger. "Boom!" the slug dropped her asshe had been struck by lightning. Another one bites the dust. Not a bad way to end a late morning hunt. Two deer down in less than 5 seconds. I climbed down the tree and walked over to examine my buck. He had a good-sized body on him and would later dress out at 150 pounds, but as I looked at his antlers, I realized that he was a basket rack 8 point. "Basket rack" means that instead of his antlers being wide and out past his ears, they were narrow and about the width of a basket ball, and fit between the buck's ears. That is probably why they call them basket racks, I don't know. Now I'll be honest, dragging those deer the 300 yards back to the truck almost killed me. Another hunter was gracious enough to help me with the second one, but it was still some work and took about 30 minutes.

As I pulled into the check station, I felt like I was on top of the world, as if I had just won the Boston Marathon. Yeah, my deer were nothing to brag about compared to some of the trophy deer that Kansas is known for, but they were *my* deer. Deer that I had gone out and killed mid-morning during the rut. It was my first and only Kansas buck so far, and I had shown that I am a hunter. You see, when I first joined the Rod and Gun Club, one of the officers asked me if I hunted. I told him yes. He asked what did I hunt, squirrels, rabbits, small game? I told him that I hunt everything. Small game, hogs, waterfowl, deer, buffalo, you name it. Another reason why I was so proud of my success is because I felt that I had to represent and prove my skills as a hunter. I was one of the very few Black members of a mostly White hunting group. I made it a point to represent and to show and prove my capabilities, because so many of the Black members seldom participated in any activities and never really made a name for themselves in the club. So as I pulled into the check station, I felt good. I dropped the tailgate and people gathered around to see what I had gotten.

"Wait, you got two?!" one of the onlookers asked me.

"Yep" I answered as I drug the deer off the tailgate.

"Where did you hunt?" another guy asked.

"Oh, I shot them back over down around that way." I told him as I pointed in a random direction being as nonspecific as I could be.

The biologist did the usual data, weight, age, etc. and I posed for a picture with both of the deer. This hunt was not only successful, but it solidified my status as a hunter within the club. Over the next few months, I would prove my abilities time and time again as a hunter, fisherman, and outdoorsman. While there were a lot of guys there that could outshoot me in skeet and sporting clays, I could hold my own when it came to hunting and fishing. In fact, it wasn't long before a friendly, not so friendly, rivalry started. Several of my coworkers and club members were keeping tabs and competing with me. It was not uncommon for some of them to stop me in the hallway and ask how many deer, or ducks I had killed so far. If their number was higher than mine, they would be ecstatic!

During a Crappiethon fishing tournament on Perry Lake a few years later, I went out in a canoe while everyone else had fancy boats with big motors and fish finders. I had an oar, a canoe, rod and reel, and some good old-fashioned luck. I stopped by two stores, but they were all sold out of minnows.

So, I was stuck with using artificial lures. The wind was so high on the lake that I was struggling to get out onto the lake and ended up fishing off of a sand bar about 200 yards from the dock. Had I gotten farther out I would have been blown all over the place in my canoe. However, when the tournament ended, I walked away with the first-place trophy. I weighed in the highest weight of fish, I think we weighed our biggest six crappie. I also caught the biggest crappie. The trophy is on my shelf to prove it. I retired the fishing lure that I used and hung it on the trophy as a reminder of what I used to further elevate my name as an outdoorsman. People were shocked and in total disbelief , but that's a story for another day. A few months later during a walleye fishing tournament, the winner of the tournament, no I didn't win this time, came looking for me. I was late returning to the dock and really had no clue about walleye fishing but I entered anyway. The guy, Tom was his name, drug that walleye all over the parking lot looking for me. Before I could even get out of the boat, I heard someone yelling "Whurs Eric?! Whurs Eric?!"

"Here I am" I told him.

"What did you catch. What did you catch?" he asked as he looked me up and down, seeing if I had any walleye, as he drug his nice- sized walleye alongside of him. He knew that I was a contender for almost everything I participated in, and if I am in a competition, there is reason to be worried.

"I didn't catch anything Tom" I've never been walleye fishing in my life until today. Looks like you caught a nice one though." I told him.

"Yep, I'm in the running for first place if nobody comes in with one bigger" Tom said.

"Well congratulations" I told him, as he walked off looking for anyone with a bigger fish.

Yes, my name and reputation was known while there on Ft, Leavenworth. and when I left, my name was on a plaque on the wall of the Rod and Gun Club. Not because of how good of a hunter I was, but for my efforts to promote hunting and membership to the Ft. Leavenworth Rod and Gun Club. As I was retiring in 2015, an incoming ILE student (Intermediate Leadership Education) stopped an asked, "Hey, you're that guy that be killing shit?" he asked.

"Yep, that would be me I told him, You've heard about me huh?" I replied.

These two deer definitely helped put my reputation on the map.

Three lessons learned from this hunt were:

1. **Trust your instincts**- While other hunters ventured farther out in search of deer, I scored big behind the skeet range by hunting in a legal area that others overlooked.

2. **Represent**- Sometimes you have to step up and show what you're capable of. Give it all you got. While it was not my intent to draw

attention to myself, or to become a legend, among hunters there on Ft, Leavenworth, I drew respect from my peers by being good at what I did.

3. **Never judge a group by its audience-**
While I was one of very few Black guys in the Rod and Gun club, I had a great time and met a lot of good people. During my own time as an ILE student, I was selected as the Student Vice President and was selected over more traditional looking hunters and outdoorsmen. This inevitably caused a friendly rivalry between me and the other nominees. It is likely that I was the first Black person ever selected to the position, and in the end, I served the Rod and Gun Club well.

Represent!

Made in the USA
Columbia, SC
18 April 2025